THROUGH THE *Valley*

MOVE YOUR LIFE FORWARD IN GOD

LAURA WOODWORTH

Through the Valley – Move Your Life Forward in God brings hope for when everything seems to be working against you. If you're stuck in a hopeless spot, Laura Woodworth compassionately meets you there and guides you back to Truth. A great resource for our times.

–Karen Bejjani, author of *The Blue Cord*, co-founder of iHOPE
　Ministries

After the last few years, I'm not sure if there's a better title for a great devotional than *Through the Valley – Move Your Life Forward in God*. Laura Woodworth is not only one of my favorite writers, but she has her finger on the pulse of where our culture is right now. If you're ready to move your life forward, I can't think of a better start than this devotional. You won't regret it.

–Phil Cooke, Ph.D., filmmaker, media executive, and author of
　*Maximize Your Influence: How to Make Digital Media Work for
　Your Church, Your Ministry, and You*

This extraordinary book gives the solid spiritual support that we all need so much in our life journey on a day-to-day basis. I am particularly impressed with the way every day's devotional in this book meets the need of my heart. One can feel God's divine guidance to the author on every page of this amazing book.

–Dr. Shurajit Gopal, Professor of Communication, North
　Greenville University

One of the most encouraging devotionals I've read in a long time! *Through the Valley – Move Your Life Forward in God* provides the reader with daily Bible reading along with an inspiring devotional that stirs a deep hope and faith in Jesus–no matter life's circumstances. As a result, I found myself focusing on the Lord more throughout my day. Thank you, Laura Woodworth, for following God's call to write a book that spurs us forward daily in our walk with Jesus.

–Carla McDougal, CEO of Reflective Media Productions, award-
　winning author of *My Prayer Chair*

This devotional is filled with revelation from the depth of God's heart for each person in everyday life experiences. The applicable steps Laura shares of freedom at the end of each devotion will minister an even greater understanding to the reader of how much they are loved by the Father. A valuable addition to your Bible study.

—Joanie Higley, prophetic intercessor

Laura's sensitive and insightful thoughts on moving your life forward will awaken something powerful in you. She's absolutely right. Life is a rollercoaster journey, and this 40-day devotional will help you through the highs and lows and keep you on track toward the places God wants to take you.

—Kathleen Cooke, co-founder of Cooke Media Group and The Influence Lab, media executive, author of *Hope 4 Today: Stay Connected to God in a Distracted Culture*

Life is a journey! What an amazing perspective to have and to live by daily. In a simple, yet very balanced approach my friend Laura has organized an awe-inspiring *map* to guide us through this journey we call LIFE. This map contains symbols and directions regarding vision, provision, trust, rest, and many more. I invite you to explore this 40-day devotional that will surely bring a renewed zest into your life journey.

—Maggie Riffler, health and wellness coach, board member of ICVM and Messenger Films

Do you feel like the Israelites wandering in the wilderness? Laura Woodworth has created a way through with the guidance of God's word to help you break out of your rut and find direction and ultimately your life purpose in this 40-day spiritual journey.

—Reneé Lawless, motivational speaker, coach, actor

Laura Woodworth is passionate about helping others to grow in our faith, be challenged to get out of our comfort zone, focus on scripture, and take action. That's what I get excited about in her new devotional *Through the Valley – Move Your Life Forward in God*. Every day you'll read scripture, pray, seek God, speak to Him and then Go Further. That's my favorite part. Don't stay where you are, but move forward, dream, look ahead, plan your next steps and then embrace everything that God has in store for you. And start with Laura's devotional!
–Karen Covell, producer and founding director, The Hollywood Prayer Network

I highly recommend *Through the Valley – Move Your Life Forward in God* by Laura Woodworth. It's a GET THROUGH IT devotional with a fresh look into our past so our future can burn brighter in front of us. Laura teaches us to relearn how to manage life in the difficult times. She reminds us that God has seen our TEARS IN A BOTTLE moments. I believe the lost DREAM will be revived by the Spirit of the Lord as you walk through this devotional. Laura has given practical and spiritual advice to reignite the gifts of God on the inside of you. You don't have to stay in the VALLEY OF DRY BONES any longer as He is prophesying over your life. I encourage you to do this devotional and allow Him to reignite the fire inside you.
–Barb Rudoski, senior co-pastor, Faith Alive Family Church, Canada

Laura Woodworth's devotional is an intelligent, well mapped out progression of growth. Unlike other devotionals that are more random in topic and layout, hers is a path through inner assessments and prayers that deepen our connection with God, freeing us to connect more with a larger life and purpose in Him.
–Isaac Hernandez, media consultant; host, *Faith on Film*

I have read many devotionals, but Laura Woodworth's *Through the Valley* devotional really spoke into my life. It was inspirational, educational and very encouraging. I look forward to reading each devotion in the 40-day journey as God reveals His grace and truth to me.
–Lori Wilke, senior co-pastor, Spirit Life Church; author, *The Costly Anointing*

ISBN: 9798218064990

Published by Family Christian Publishing, 2555 Northwinds Parkway, Alpharetta, GA 30009.

A FREE GIFT FOR YOU

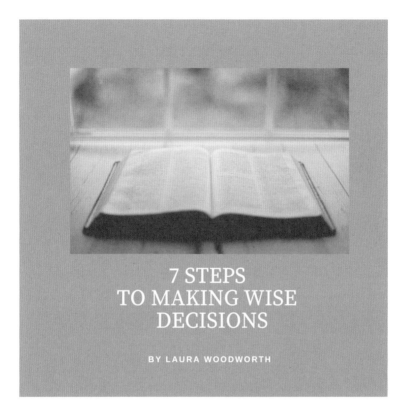

Moving your life forward involves making wise, godly decisions.

"7 Steps to Making Wise Decisions" will help you hear God's voice and discover his guidance through scripture. I've found that readers who download this free resource are better equipped to take the next steps in their spiritual journey.

If you don't have a copy, you can get it for free here:

https://www.laurawoodworth.com/free-download

*Dedicated to the One
who calls us by name.*

Table of Contents

Preface: Welcome to the Journey

How to Get the Most Out of This Journey

WELCOME TO THE JOURNEY

Dear friend,

Do you ever feel like there is something more to life? Deep down inside, you sense something new and exciting is just around the bend if you could only move past your grief or recover your momentum...

Life is a journey. In its biggest picture, it's a journey from the womb to the grave and then on into eternity. Along the way, it's an adventure that takes you through valleys, over rivers and across deserts. For those who put their trust in God, it's a narrow path that ultimately winds upward into mountain heights.

It's a journey with a promise.

Where are you on this journey? If you've found yourself in a valley, whether through grief or pain or simply a loss of vision, *Through the Valley – Move Your Life Forward in God* will take you from where you are in your spiritual walk to a life of greater freedom and purpose.

You'll discover places in your soul you've never opened to God before and experience his deep healing and empowering strength. This 40-day devotional will be the compassionate hand-up or the friendly push to get your life back into gear so you can move through your valley into the promising future God has for you, that wonderful "something" that is just around the bend.

Are you ready to begin? I'm praying good things for you as you journey forward.

Laura Woodworth

HOW TO GET THE MOST OUT OF THIS JOURNEY

Through the Valley – Move Your Life Forward in God is designed as a 40-day journey of discovery. Each day's reading is based on scripture and includes prayers, prophetic proclamations, and questions to help you consider where you are in your Christian walk, help you receive God's healing and empowering, and then guide you forward into the good future God has for you.

At the end of this 40-day journey, out of the valley will emerge a new and stronger "you" with vision for your future. You'll be motivated and empowered to move towards it.

Daily Scripture: Write it on a sticky note, hide it in your heart! These Bible verses bring the truth of God's word into your situation. You'll be strengthened, inspired and encouraged on your journey forward.

Daily Reading: Open your heart to receive all that God has for you. Ask the Holy Spirit to teach you and guide you into truth as you read.

Pray: Ask and it shall be given to you. Each day's simple prayer offers an opportunity to ask for God's help to become all he has called you to be.

Seek: These questions will help you ponder and examine your life. They are opportunities to gain true self-awareness—to evaluate where you are, where you want to go, and what it will take to get there. Think of these as "action steps" to help you apply the day's concept.

Speak: We believe what we hear ourselves say. This is your opportunity to speak the word of God over your life—to prophesy to your spirit! The Bible is living and active. When you apply it and declare God's truths over your life, the results will be amazing.

Go further: Additional scripture references will help you delve deeper into Bible truths. Let God's truth set you free to pursue your future in him with joy and great abandonment.

"When they walk through the Valley of Weeping, it will become a place of refreshing springs, where pools of blessing collect after the rains."

PSALM 84:6 NLT

DAY 1

FIRST THINGS FIRST—VISION

*W*hat's your valley? Is it grief? Depression? Or, if you're honest with yourself, is it a place of wandering? Perhaps you've lost your vision and now you're just going through the motions until something changes—retirement hits or the kids move out or that perfect job or spouse comes along.

Life is a journey. Your Christian walk can be an immensely fulfilling adventure—a pilgrimage from who you are to the person God has called you to become. If you've missed this concept, it's easy for your life to be stalemated. Vision lost, momentum gone... But God has not called you to wander in this valley; he's called you to move forward into the fullness of life found in Jesus Christ.

There's a calling on your life, a reason for living. Let's look further into Psalm 84...

"Happy are those who are strong in the Lord, who set their minds on a pilgrimage to Jerusalem. When they walk through the Valley of Weeping, it will become a place of refreshing springs, where pools of blessing collect after the rains! They will continue to grow stronger, and each of them will appear before God in Jerusalem" (Psalm 84:5-7 NLT).

Did you notice the "walk through" part of this scripture? Your valley may mean healing or rest or a pause in the chaos of life, but it is something you were meant to travel through. The beautiful thing is that as you step forward, strength, blessing and refreshment will come with plenty to spare for others.

It's time to move your life forward. It's time to lift your eyes and see the way ahead.

I pray God will restore your vision and purpose for living. May you have the grace and strength to move your life towards the beautiful destiny you have in God. This is your opportunity to live the life he has always envisioned for you.

Pray

"God, help me fully grasp my purpose for living.
Give me the grace and strength to step towards
my future today. In Jesus' name, amen."

Seek

What's your valley?
Do you believe God can
turn it into blessing? Take
a moment and entrust this
valley into God's hands.

_____

_____

_____

_____

_____

_____

Speak

I am blessed and refreshed in God. I am growing stronger in him.

_____

_____

_____

_____

_____

_____

_____

_____

Go further

Psalm 84, 2 Corinthians 1:3-4, John 10:10

"Even when I walk through the dark valley of death, I will not be afraid, for you are close beside me. Your rod and your staff protect and comfort me."

PSALM 23:4 NLT

NEVER ALONE

Why do children always ask for "one more" story at bedtime? One more book to read or song to sing, anything to prolong the time before you turn off the light and leave them alone in the dark.

We don't like the dark. We avoid dark alleys, dark rooms, dark hallways. And yet, at times we must walk the dark valley of death. Your valley may be the passing of a spouse or close friend or family pet. It could be a difficult diagnosis like cancer or infertility that throws you into the darkness. Or, it could be the death of a dream, a marriage, the hope you had for the future.

As human beings, we're most vulnerable in the dark. Our eyes adjust but not enough to discern the moving shadows. Our ears may detect movement but without sight, it's difficult to define the threat. I do not claim to know your darkness, but I know Someone whose understanding is infinite. He will never leave you alone, even in the darkest valley. In those moments, your spiritual senses must prevail.

Close your eyes a moment. In your dark valley, can you sense the Lord? Can you see him with the rod and staff in his hand ready to defend you from the thieves and raiders hiding in the shadows? Can you imagine his towering presence protecting, calming and comforting you?

When everything around you is dark, the Bible reminds us that God is light. To him, the night shines as bright as day. Nothing—absolutely nothing—can separate you from his presence and help.

You are never alone, even in the dark night of your soul. Take courage and keep moving forward.

And I am convinced that nothing can ever separate us from God's love. Neither death nor life, neither angels nor demons, neither our fears for today nor our worries about tomorrow—not even the powers of hell can separate us from God's love" (Romans 8:38 NLT).

Pray

> "God, come and enter my darkness. Shine your light
> and surround me with your goodness. I believe you
> are with me. In Jesus' name, amen."

Seek

What is the darkness in your life?
Has a loved one passed, or
is it a dream that has died?
Take a moment now to let the
Lord's comfort and light flood
into that dark place.

I will not be afraid because God is with me.
Nothing can separate me from his presence.

Go further

"Dear friends, don't be surprised at the fiery trials you are going through, as if something strange were happening to you."

1 PETER 4:12 NLT

HELP IS ON THE WAY

*N*ow that we've embarked on this journey together, I have one disclaimer: your journey forward may not be easy. It may be very, very hard. Trials will come. Your faith will be tested. One foot out the door and your coffee spills or the car won't start. Or worse yet, a loved one gets a bad diagnosis, your workplace starts laying off employees, or your child is bullied at school.

Life can be challenging. As you determine to move forward into the fullness of God's purpose, it can feel like the enemy is waging an all-out war against you—anything to push you back and slow you down in this journey.

But I'm here to tell you that help is on the way. Can you believe that? Can you stir hope and faith and lift your eyes to where your help comes from? In the midst of life's challenges, it's important to consider what you believe...

Either God heals the brokenhearted—or he doesn't.
Either he saves to the uttermost—or he doesn't.
Either he sets the captive free—or he doesn't.
Either he watches over his word to fulfill it in the earth—or he doesn't.

What do you believe?

The enemy of your soul is hard at work in the earth and there is a very real battle waging in the heavenlies over your faith and loyalty. It's important to decide now how you will approach life.

When life seems to be crumbling around you, will you stand in faith, trusting God to keep his word and his promises? Or will you allow yourself to wallow in doubt and despair, wavering in every difficult situation—always questioning God's word and never fully believing?

The Bible tells us that God's word will not return void. In other words, it will accomplish what he has sent it forth to do: saving, healing, blessing, guiding. Don't let your current circumstances or what you see in front of you prevent you from trusting the Lord and his promises. Help is on the way. Keep moving forward in faith.

Pray

> "God, I believe your word. I ask for your help to press through every challenge and gain the victory you have for me. In Jesus' name, amen."

Seek

What is your biggest challenge today?
What is God's word concerning it? Seek out a promise from the Bible for your situation, then pray for his help and believe.

God is my savior. He is my healer and my deliverer in every situation.

Go further

1 Peter 4:7-10, Psalm 147:3, Luke 4:18, Isaiah 55:11,
Ephesians 6:10-18

"You have turned my mourning into joyful dancing. You have taken away my clothes of mourning and clothed me with joy."

PSALM 30:11 NLT

TEARS IN A BOTTLE

There is a time for grieving, a time for weeping. The saying "buck up" and be strong doesn't always apply. Sometimes you need to give in to the tears and weep.

Perhaps a loved one has passed or you've come to the sudden realization that you've missed a moment that will never come your way again. You said no to a relationship and years later, you're still alone. You've passed the age of childbearing with no child in your arms. You're stuck with a regret that can never be righted as you lay a parent in the grave. The sorrow is threatening to overwhelm you.

God knows.

He keeps track of all your sorrows. The Bible says, "You have collected all my tears in your bottle. You have recorded each one in your book" (Psalm 56:8 NLT). And it also says that he will turn your sorrow into joy, your mourning into dancing.

How is that possible? You know it will take a miracle. Something only God can do.

The Israelites knew what it was like for the impossible to be made possible. Manna in the desert. Water from a rock. Divine provision in a dry and barren wilderness.

Numbers 21 describes the Israelites' journey from Moab to Beer through the desert. The people despaired of life itself with no water in sight, nothing to quench their overwhelming thirst. God told Moses to gather the people together and he would give them water. A well of refreshing. A miracle.

Their mourning was turned into joy. Their desperate situation was eased with God's provision. It was there that the Israelites sang, "Spring up, O well! Yes, sing its praises!" (Numbers 21:17 NLT).

God can do that for you. He can cause springs of life to bubble up in your soul. It begins by entrusting your deepest sorrow to the One who can work the miraculous. And then maybe, just maybe, the time for dancing will begin.

Pray

> *"God, I desperately need your touch and your help.
> I turn my sorrow over to you and I ask for a miracle of joy."*

Seek

**Is sadness overwhelming
your soul?**
Open your heart and pour
out your sorrow before the
Lord. Then ask him to turn
your sorrow into joy.

Spring up, O well of God! Spring up in me.

Go further

Isaiah 35, Psalm 126:5, Psalm 51:12, Numbers 21:16-18

"You make springs pour water into the ravines, so streams gush down from the mountains."

PSALM 104:10 NLT

YOU ARE NOT FORGOTTEN

*A*t times, your journey through the valley may feel bleak and lonely, especially if you're struggling with grief, an extended illness, or a destructive dependency you're trying to break. Over time it can alienate others.

Sometimes even the most well-meaning people want you to move past loss quickly—too quickly—or they're unable to empathize with your battle over addiction. One by one, they drift away, weary of your struggle, afraid of the demands on the friendship as you continue to wrestle through, struggling to find your way to victory.

But you are not forgotten. You are not alone. As King David declared in his moments of darkness, "Even when I walk through the dark valley of death, I will not be afraid, for you are close beside me" (Psalm 23:4 NLT).

Though others may desert you, God is always near. A beautiful thing can happen in your life when you fully grasp this truth. An exchange can occur—your grief for his joy. Your chaos for his peace. Your reliance on harmful coping mechanisms for a complete and utter dependency on the God of your salvation, the One who holds your life in his hands.

You are not forgotten and he is not rushing you. God always allows you time to figure life out. He doesn't rush the healing process, but he does send Holy Spirit nudges as reminders that your current struggle—your dark valley—is a "walk through," not a "settling in" place. What you are living through right now is not your forever reality.

If you're feeling alone or forgotten, look up. Look at the beautiful reminders of God's care in his creation—the stars in the sky, the streams that pour down into the valley to refresh and renew. I speak God's refreshing into your soul. I pray you can sense his very nearness. You are not alone.

Pray

> *"God, I thank you that you are close to me in this dark valley. I receive your streams of refreshing. Help me find the path to victory, in Jesus' holy name, amen."*

Seek

What are you struggling with in life?

Is it loss? Sickness? A destructive dependency? Commit your grief or your struggle into God's hands now and trust him for his help.

Speak

I am not alone in this valley. God is close by.

Go further

Isaiah 61:1-3, Psalm 104:1-10, John 14:25-27

"He has paid
a full ransom
for his people."

PSALM 111:9 NLT

ARE YOU HIDING SOMETHING?

*Y*ou don't have to look far in our society to find someone who has suffered at the hands of wickedness. Prejudice, discrimination, verbal and physical abuse or molestation can lead to feelings of shame—even when you're not at fault.

If it's happened to you, your first response may be to cover it up, pretend it never happened, and somehow limp along in life, hiding your pain and anger. You may even wonder how God could have let this happen, but you must remember that God does not force people to love him. He has given every person free will to choose between good and evil. Unfortunately, you have been caught in the fray of this spiritual battle.

The Bible tells us about Tamar, a daughter of King David. She was beautiful and her half-brother Amnon was desperately in love with her. He deceived her by creating a situation where they were alone together, then strong-armed and molested her. Once the act was done, he despised her and kicked her to the street.

She could have slunk home in disgrace, but instead, Tamar tore her beautiful robe and put ashes on her head in mourning as she went out into the public streets. The deed was out in the open.

A wound can heal when it is exposed to sunlight and air.

You are valuable to God. If you have suffered abuse or injustice, this evil was not his plan and will be accounted for. God has paid a full ransom to free you from any shame, guilt or anger you might feel.

As a good shepherd, God is in this valley to anoint your head and your heart with healing oil. Bring your pain out in the open and allow his healing to soak into your life. Let God make you whole again.

Pray

"God, come to me today. Cleanse me from evil and
free me from the shame I have endured.
I receive your healing oil now, in Jesus' name."

Seek

**Have you been abused or
mistreated?**
How so? Today, seek out the
Lord and seek the help you
need for healing.* Don't let
someone else's evil deed
define your life.

*If you are in a life-threatening situation, get out and get help. Jesus already died for that
person; you don't have to.*

Speak

I am valuable to God. He has ransomed my life from the evil one.

Go further

John 16:33, Psalm 23:4-5, Luke 4:18-19

"If God is for us, who
can be against us?"

ROMANS 8:31 NIV

IS GOD MAD AT YOU?

*H*ave you ever wondered if God is mad at you? Maybe that's why the washer keeps breaking or your bank account is always overdrawn. You take a step forward and it feels like you get pushed two steps back. You're beginning to wonder if it's God's "punishment" for some unaccounted sin.

The Pharisees cornered Jesus one Sabbath, hoping to accuse him of sin. They set him up by bringing a man into the synagogue with a deformity. Would Jesus heal him? In their eyes, the act of healing would be "work" that violated the Sabbath law, giving them the legal right to condemn Jesus.

The man was desperate, his life disabled by the withered hand. Jesus "turned to his critics and asked, 'Is it legal to do good deeds on the Sabbath, or is it a day for doing harm? Is this a day to save life or destroy it?'"

 The Pharisees gave no response. The Bible tells us that Jesus "looked around at them angrily, because he was deeply disturbed by their hard hearts…" (Mark 3:4,5 NLT)

Jesus reached out in compassion and healed the man that day. The calloused Pharisees went away from the miracle even more determined to kill Jesus.

It was not their sin that angered Jesus most that day. It was the hard heart behind the sin—the callousness that can't see a need, embrace a miracle or rejoice in God's goodness.

Are you hard-hearted? Have you allowed bitterness, anger or revenge to take root in your soul? The Pharisees were blinded by their hardness of heart. You don't have to be.

If you've grown calloused, repent and be healed. Return to God. He is slow to anger and abounding in love! He is for you and not against you.

Pray

"God, I confess that I have become calloused. Create in me a clean heart. Renew a right spirit in me. In Jesus' name, amen."

Seek

Has your heart grown hard?
What has caused that hardness? Repent and receive God's healing for your heart. Then trust his goodness towards you!

Speak

God is for me and not against me.

Go further

Joel 2:12-13, Psalm 51:10, Matthew 5:8

"The eyes of the Lord watch over those who do right; his ears are open to their cries for help."

PSALM 34:15 NLT

PROVISION AND PROTECTION IN THE VALLEY

*I*t was an honorable mission. Threatened by the king of Moab, the kings of Israel and Judah set out with their armies to confront the enemy. But the ourney was long and their troops and horses languished from thirst. They would die on this mission unless God intervened.

"'What should we do?' the king of Israel cried out. 'The Lord has brought the three of us here to let the king of Moab defeat us'" (2 Kings 3:10 NLT).

Desperately, they cried to God for help. And miraculously, God sent divine provision. Overnight, the valley before them filled with water, not from rain or wind but from a supernatural supply. The need was met; disaster was prevented. But the miracle wasn't over.

When the enemy army saw the pools of water, they thought it was blood. Believing that the Israelite armies had turned on each other, the Moabites went out to seize the plunder. To their surprise, the Israelite armies attacked and won a great victory. (2 Kings 3:10-27).

Your situation may seem dire and impossible. You may have started on this Christian journey with zeal and great hope, but the journey has been long. You've wandered into a valley that seems endless, and you're weary and thirsty and at your wits' end.

You desperately need God's provision and protection as old enemies of your soul raise their ugly heads, taunting you and threatening your resolve to live for the Lord.

God displayed his glory for the Israelite kings. He sent provision and protection and a mighty victory over their enemy. And he will do the same for you. Seek the Lord. Ask for his help and trust in his salvation.

Pray

> "Help, God! I need your provision and protection from the enemies that are rising against me. Come now and save me. In Jesus' name, I ask, amen."

Seek

What is your greatest need right now?
Ask the Lord for his help and listen closely for his response.

Speak

I depend on God. He is my help. He is my protection and provision.

Go further

Psalm 33:18-20, Psalm 121, Matthew 6:31-33

"*My sheep listen to my voice...*"

JOHN 10:27 NLT

WHO ARE YOU LISTENING TO?

Did you know that God is always speaking? Speaking faith, speaking hope, speaking life. But we can slip into despair when life looks impossible, when things we hoped and dreamed for look unachievable and the enemy is whispering, "Just quit. Give it up."

The Gospel of Mark talks about a "give it up" kind of situation. Jairus, the ruler of the Jewish synagogue, was frantic. His little girl was dying. Desperate, he pushed through the crowds and fell before Jesus, begging him to come and lay his hands on his daughter. He believed Jesus could save her when nothing else had.

Imagine the surge of relief and joy Jairus felt when Jesus agreed to go with him. But on the way, another desperate person interrupted their progress. Sick for 12 years, the woman had spent all she had on doctors with no improvement. Like Jairus, she had faith. If she could only touch the hem of Jesus' clothes, she would be healed. When she touched Jesus' robe, she was.

Even as her miracle happened, messengers from Jairus's house arrived with horrible news. "'Your daughter is dead,' they said. 'Why bother the teacher anymore?'" Jesus overheard them and said to Jairus, "'Don't be afraid; just believe'" (Mark 5:35, 36 NIV).

You may be at a low point. The very real facts of life may be staring you in the face—impending bankruptcy, a foster child situation that's not working out, a marriage that is failing.

But nothing is impossible with God. Jairus's daughter was healed that day—miraculously brought back from the dead because her father believed the words of life instead of the "facts" of the matter.

Don't be afraid. Listen closely for the Good Shepherd's voice. Your miracle may look different than you first imagined, but God's word is always "believe." Today may be your miracle day.

Pray

"God, help me to hear your voice. Help me to have faith and believe for _____. In Jesus' name, amen."

Seek

What miracle do you need?
Seek God's word for your situation, believe it, then speak it over your life.

Speak

I believe God's word in my situation. I speak life!

Go further

Mark 5:21-43, John 11:17-44,
Genesis 18:13-24, Psalm 149:6

"For the glory of your name, O Lord, save me. In your righteousness, bring me out of this distress."

PSALM 143:11 NLT

A BUMP IN THE ROAD

*H*ave you hit a bump in your road? Just when you were getting your stride, you've tripped and now it seems like you've landed in a bottomless pit with no way out. It can happen to the best of us.

The prophet Jeremiah ended up in a pit and Joseph did too. Two God-fearing men left to die—Jeremiah in a dungeon filled with muck and mire; Joseph in a well, tossed there by his brothers. There was really no hope for either of them.

They had done nothing wrong. There was no deep hidden sin that God was punishing them for. Yet, there they were, stuck in a place where there was no getting out of—but for God.

What was on Jeremiah's mind as he sank into the mire at the bottom of the dungeon? What thoughts plagued Joseph as he looked up the slick walls of the well? It would have been easy to grow bitter.

It took 30 men to drag Jeremiah out of the muddy pit. Joseph was pulled out by his brothers only to be sold as a slave—which ultimately paved the way for him to become the prince of Egypt, assuring the salvation of his entire family in a time of severe famine.

Joseph's attitude was portrayed when his brothers arrived in Egypt to buy grain. As they bowed low before him, he revealed his identity and acknowledged God's presence in that dark pit they had tossed him into.

"'But don't be upset, and don't be angry with yourselves for selling me to this place. It was God who sent me here ahead of you to preserve your lives'" (Genesis 45:5 NLT). At that moment, the enslaved one became their deliverer.

I don't know what your pit, your deep dark valley may be, but I do know that God is there with you and he can turn your situation around. Your life is in his hands. Rescue is on the way.

Pray

"God, you are the only one who can save me.
I lift my eyes to you and ask you to rescue me.
In Jesus' name, I pray, amen."

Seek

Are you in a distressing situation?
If something has tripped you up,
cry out to God for his rescue and
believe that this situation will be
turned to his glory.

Speak

God is my rescue. I declare that he will be glorified through this trial.

Go further

Psalm 71:2-3, Jeremiah 38:6-13, Genesis 37:18-28

"The Lord is my strength and my song; he has become my victory... I will not die, but I will live to tell what the Lord has done."

PSALM 118:14, 17 NLT

A WAY THROUGH

*A*re you stuck? Stuck in a dead-end job, stuck in a relationship gone bad, stuck in a house that turned into more than you can handle? Or maybe you've lost a loved one or lost a friendship through a tragic misunderstanding. Now *you* feel lost, in limbo and without purpose. Possibly even hopeless.

Depression has a way of finding you in these situations. Like a mist that settles into a valley, the oppression envelopes you, so thick you can't see your way through. Like sleep overtakes a person in the final stages of hypothermia, you are slowly succumbing to the dark numbness, the shroud of depression.

We all face times of sadness. It's a natural part of the life cycle. The mistake comes when you settle into those dark valleys of the soul and take up residence... or when they take residence in you. You err when you embrace the idea that this is all there is, and in that belief, stop moving, stop pursuing something more–a way out, a way through.

Valleys like this are a walk of faith, a testing of your belief system. Either God is good... or he's not. Either there is something bright ahead in your future... or this is all there is. Remember, this is a pilgrimage with a promise.

"Happy are those who are strong in the Lord, who set their minds on a pilgrimage to Jerusalem. When they walk through the Valley of Weeping, it will become a place of refreshing springs where pools of blessing collect after the rains! They will continue to grow stronger..." (Psalm 84:5-7a NLT).

It's in these moments of despair that you must strengthen yourself in the Lord. Throw off the heaviness, throw off the shroud. Pull your hiking boots back on and set your mind to walk. Step by step, find your way forward and through this valley.

As you do, the tears you've cried will somehow miraculously accumulate as pools of blessing. Joy will return. Strength will come back as you determine to find your way forward. Trust God in this and you will find your way through to brighter days.

Pray

*"Lord, come be my strength and my song.
Refresh my life! I throw off depression and
declare my victory in you. Amen."*

Seek

**What is making you feel stuck
or weighed down?**
Bring it before the Lord, then
stir your faith and set your
mind to move forward. Trust
him for new strength.

God is my strength and my song! He is my victory.

Go further

Psalm 118:14-17, John 11:43-44, Psalm 23:6

"I am waiting for you, O Lord. You must answer for me, O Lord my God."

PSALM 38:15 NLT

TURN A DEAF EAR

*Y*ou may have been in this valley a long time, believing, praying, even excitedly anticipating an answer to a prayer or a miracle in a seemingly impossible situation… but nothing seems to budge. You feel a little foolish for hanging on for so long and now the enemy is talking.

"You'll never be healed. Just live with it."
"You'll be in this dead-end job forever."
"You'll never get out of this situation. Own it."
"Give in and quit dreaming. Who are you anyway?"

Waiting can be hard. The longer you wait, the louder the doubts. The enemy is working hard to rattle your cage, shake your faith, undermine everything you've been working towards.

King David faced great opposition in his lifetime. The fact that David knew he was not without sin added ammunition to the taunts and threats of the enemies he faced. He had committed adultery and then placed the woman's husband in the thick of battle where he would undoubtedly be killed (2 Samuel 11). Afterward, David's repentance was heartfelt, but the facts of what he had done were still out there—fodder for the devil's tactics to trip him up and pull him down.

And yet, there was an unshakeable faith inside King David, a deep trust that no matter how dark life seemed, God was on his side.

"I am deaf to all their threats," King David said, referring to the taunts of the enemy. "I choose to hear nothing, and I make no reply" (Psalm 38:13,14 NLT).

What enabled him to be so steadfast in the face of the enemy? How could he resist the urge to respond or cave to the enemy's goading? He had committed himself to God. He looked to the only One who could save him.

When life seems bleak and nothing seems to be moving, you can either cave in to the voices of doubt or choose to believe God's word over your life. You will move through this valley. Trust and believe.

Pray

> "Dear God, you are my defense. I choose to believe
> your word over my life. I will press forward into the future
> you have prepared for me. In Jesus' name, amen."

Seek

**Is there unconfessed sin in
your life?**
Don't give the enemy anything
to use against you. Confess your
sin now, seek God's forgiveness
and move forward.

Speak

When the enemy taunts me, I choose
to hear nothing. I choose to believe God.

Go further

Psalm 38, 1 John 1:5-9, Psalm 43:1-3

"The Lord is not slow in keeping His promise as some understand slowness, but is patient with you, not wanting anyone to perish but everyone to come to repentance."

2 PETER 3:9 BSB

A VALLEY OF PRAYER

*I*s your valley one of prayer and intercession? Are you carrying the heavy burden of a family member in need of salvation? Their life hangs between heaven and hell and the weightiness almost overwhelms you. You're wondering when or even if the victory will be won.

You firmly believe the word of God for their life—a life filled with the peace and joy of God's salvation. It's just that it's been so very long. Your prayers seem to be hitting a glass ceiling. Nothing seems to be changing; nothing seems to be moving.

I'm here to encourage you. Don't give up. Don't stop praying. Keep interceding and believing and sowing for their salvation. We don't always know what is happening in the spiritual heavenlies where the life and death battle is being fought.

It may seem like the enemy is gaining ground in that person's life, but I'm here to remind you that the Stronger One is here. Jesus has come to seek and save the lost. He desires everyone to come to repentance.

You may not fully understand all that is at stake or *how many* lives are at stake, inexplicably entwined with the one person you are travailing for in prayer. You may think you're saving one life when in reality, countless lives hang in the balance.

The Bible says that one man can put a thousand to flight and two can put ten thousand to flight (Deuteronomy 32:30). While it may feel like you are alone in your prayers, others may be praying as well and the compound effect of those prayers will be exponential.

As you travel the valley of this deep intercession, trust that your prayers have effect. Trust that God is at work. Believe that your travail will turn into the triumph of a beautifully redeemed life.

Pray

> *"God, I believe you answer prayer. I ask you to save and deliver _____. Free them from the devil's grip and help them come to repentance and faith in you. In Jesus' name, amen."*

Seek

Can you identify the strongholds that have gripped your friend or loved one?

Use this discernment to break the enemy's grip as you pray for their salvation.

Speak

I declare that Jesus is the Stronger One in _____'s life.
I declare that _____ belongs to the Lord and that God's
salvation is at work in their life.

Go further

1 Corinthians 15:57-58, Luke 19:9-10, James 5:16

"Who can list the glorious miracles of the Lord? Who can ever praise him half enough?"

PSALM 106:2 NLT

ARE YOU TESTING GOD'S PATIENCE?

*A*re you testing God's patience? Have you lost your momentum? Most of us know the story of the Israelites, God's people who were enslaved in Egypt for over 400 years. At their cries of groaning, God sent Moses and rescued them from their bondage with tremendous miracles and the promise of a good land, a land of "milk and honey."

Yet the Bible says the people were unimpressed with God's miracles. Sure, they rejoiced after they crossed the Red Sea on dry ground and then watched the waters rush back in, destroying their enemies. But afterward, they quickly turned away from the Lord.

The Bible recounts, "Yet how quickly they forgot what he had done! They wouldn't wait for his counsel! In the wilderness, their desires ran wild, testing God's patience in that dry land."

The sad story continues, "They traded their glorious God for a statue of a grass-eating bull! They forgot God, their savior…" (Psalm 106:13-14, 20-21 NLT).

Ultimately, they refused to enter the promised land and wandered in a desert for 40 years.

What are you doing in this valley? If it's turned dry and desperate and if the promised land seems to have moved out of reach, it's a good time to check your faith. Have you forgotten the faithfulness of God and turned aside to careless desires or lazy living? Have you discounted his goodness and through unbelief, exchanged your relationship with the living God for the ways of the world?

These are tough questions to ask, but if you've lost the vision and the desire to move towards the wonderful promises of God, you've got to look deep inside. If you've grown doubtful in this journey, remember the miracles. Remember the faithfulness of God and be thankful. Regain your momentum by praising God for his goodness.

Pray

> "God, I confess my unbelief. Help me to believe in all your good promises! Save me out of this valley and help me move forward into your promised land. In Jesus' name, amen."

Seek

Have you discredited God's goodness in your life?
Make a list of the good things he has done in your life so far. Praise him for those things and regain your forward movement.

_____

_____

_____

_____

_____

Speak

I will not forget. I will praise the Lord for all his goodness towards me.

_____

_____

_____

_____

_____

_____

_____

_____

Go further

Psalm 106, Mark 9:21-24, 2 Timothy 2:21-23

"... *He who has begun a good work in you will complete it until the day of Jesus Christ.*"

PHILIPPIANS 1:6 NKJV

WHEN A DREAM
(OR SOMEONE YOU LOVE) DIES

Some valleys are valleys of death—desert land, dry and dusty with no signs of life. The heat is oppressive and your thirst unquenchable. It's not you who died, but it's you who now have to find a way to get on with the business of living.

Psychologists tell us there are five stages of grief: denial, anger, bargaining, depression, and finally acceptance. Acceptance that someone or *something* has died. For you, it may be a literal death in the family. For someone else, it may be the death of a dream or a relationship or an opportunity.

No matter what has brought you to this place of grief, this wrestling with death and dying, I'd like to suggest a sixth stage of the grief process: Joy.

I'm not at all making light of the grief process. Trying to "move on" with life without acknowledging your loss can regrettably create more pain down the road.

However, you're doing yourself and those around you a huge disservice if you never go beyond the stage of acceptance. Like the widow who lives the rest of her life in black mourning clothes, you close the door on God's intention for your life—to be blessed and to be a blessing.

It takes an act of faith to move forward. It takes a deep belief in God's purpose and calling to throw off the grave clothes and dust off your dreams. Despite the loss, despite the disappointment, you must believe that God is not finished yet. There is a good work he wants to do in you and through you.

There is joy ahead if you are ready to step into your future. Stir your faith and believe.

Pray

"God, I cry out to you for help! Come, Lord. Take my grief and my sadness and turn it into joy. In Jesus' name, amen."

Seek

Are you grieving?
Are you stuck in acceptance mode? Commit your loss—whether it is a loved one or a dream—into God's hands and believe for the future.

Speak

God is not finished with me yet. He who
began a good work in me will complete it!

Go further

Psalm 30, Psalm 4:6-7, John 15:11

"No longer do I call you servants, for a servant does not know what his master is doing; but I have called you friends..."

JOHN 15:15 NKJV

ARE YOU LONELY?

*A*re you lonely? We live in a lonely society, often made lonelier by the passing of a loved one or a beloved pet, and most recently, heightened by the waves of the 2020 pandemic and its ensuing restrictions.

Sometimes an illness can separate you from others, especially if it's chronic. Your friends and family may have been there at the start to support you, but a long-term illness drains everyone. At some point, people have to tend to their own life or family needs.

No matter how you've ended up in this lonely state, you have two choices. The first is to fill your life with mindless TV and food binges, or the slippery slide of drugs and alcohol—anything to numb your pain. The second (and better choice) is to seize the moment and seek the Lord.

God longs for a relationship with you. Remember the Garden of Eden story when God came looking for Adam? "And they heard the sound of the Lord God walking in the garden in the cool of the day… Then the Lord God called to Adam and said to him, 'Where are you?'" (Genesis 3:8-9 NKJV).

Adam was hiding because he had sinned. But can you imagine, right here and now, the Lord walking in your valley, seeking you out just to spend a little time with you? To fill the void and heal the ache of loneliness?

So often we put God out of reach in the heavens, sitting unapproachably on his throne. He is high and lifted up, but he is also the One who…

- Draws people to himself (John 6:44).
- Calls you by name (Isaiah 43:1).
- Calls you his friend (John 15:15).

In your lonely valley, draw near to God. Listen for his voice as he calls out for you. Use these quiet moments to cultivate friendship with the living God. Out of that relationship will spring life so you, in turn, can ease the loneliness of another on this journey. The world can be a lonely place, but you don't have to settle for a lonely future.

Pray

> *"God, I need you. Come and fill the loneliness in my heart and help me in turn to be a friend to others. In Jesus' name, amen."*

Seek

Are you lonely?
How can you counteract that loneliness? Determine now to cultivate your relationship with God and build lasting friendships with others.

Speak

I am never alone. God knows my name and he calls me friend.

Go further

Isaiah 43:1-2, John 15:15-16, Matthew 28:19-20

"I press on, that I may lay hold of that for which Christ Jesus has also laid hold of me."

PHILIPPIANS 3:12 NKJV

PRESS ON

The apostle Paul was under home arrest when he wrote this scripture. His future was uncertain and incredibly bleak. He had been beaten, stoned, whipped and imprisoned multiple times. Yet he still endured. He stayed true to the course God laid out for him.

The scripture continues, "Brethren, I do not count myself to have apprehended; but one thing I do, forgetting those things which are behind and reaching forward to those things which are ahead, I press toward the goal for the prize of the upward call of God in Christ Jesus" (Philippians 3:13-14 NKJV).

Does your journey—this valley—seem endless? Although you may not be in prison, your life may seem as bleak as Paul's. You've been working hard and giving your goals and dreams all you've got, yet it's hard to see the light at the end of the tunnel, let alone believe there even *is* an end to it.

You may be fighting off hopelessness. Perhaps you've toyed with—or been plagued by—the idea of giving up. Turning in your walking stick and calling it quits. You might even be wondering if it's worth it to face another day.

Press on.

Can you hear Paul as he looks over the rim of heaven to call out to you? Press on! It's worth it! "Stand fast in the Lord, beloved" (Philippians 4:1 NKJV).

When your valley seems longest, when everything in you is ready to toss in the towel, press on. Stay true to the course God has laid out for you, the reason he has called you out of darkness and into his light. Reach towards it! Believe for it!

Forget the toil and trouble of yesterday. Believe God's truth that as you continue to sow good things, you will reap a reward. You will see a harvest. Keep working toward that day when you will finally be all that Christ Jesus saved you for, the reason he laid hold of your life. Press on.

Pray

> *"Jesus, help me to keep pressing into who you are and all that you have for me. Help me to believe and reach for it! In your name, I pray."*

Seek

Have you been tempted to give up?

Do you believe God has called you to this? Encourage your faith by writing down the fruit you will gain as you work towards the goal.

Speak

I will not give up! I press forward into all that God has for my life.

Go further

Proverbs 14:23, Galatians 6:7-8, 1 Corinthians 3:5-7

"... the snare has been broken, and we have escaped! Our help is in the name of the Lord, the Maker of heaven and earth."

PSALM 124:7-8 NIV

SET FREE

*W*e all go through valley experiences, but some of us seem to be forever chained to them. No matter how hard you try to believe, it's like you've been tied to a tree and can't break free, forever a prisoner to generational sins, bad decisions, attitudes and oppressive thought patterns that bleed over into the rest of your life. As soon as you seem to make a little headway, something yanks your chain and pulls you back.

You've come to the awful realization that your life will never play out the way it should—the good way God intended—if you don't break free. This is one valley you will never get out of if the enemy of your soul has his way.

The Israelites endured some very desperate situations. Their history is riddled with times of wandering, imprisonment and suffering, often because of their rebellion against God but many times simply because of the spiritual warfare of this world.

They were shackled. Sometimes the chains were literal iron chains and sometimes it was the spiritual shackling of their impoverished souls. But in their oppression, they realized their only hope of deliverance was from God. They knew the best thing to do was cry out to God.

"'Lord, help!' they cried in their trouble, and he saved them from their distress… he snapped their chains… He broke down their prison gates of bronze; he cut apart their bars of iron… He spoke, and they were healed—snatched from the door of death" (Psalm 107:13-20 NLT).

What if I told you that you could be free? All it takes is a cry, a shout for help.

Your shackles can be broken. Your help is in the name of the Lord. Shout now. Cry out now. Speak to those areas of captivity in your life and declare deliverance to your soul. The blood of Jesus Christ has broken every snare and you can go free.

Pray

> "God, I cry to you for help. I ask you to break off every chain in my life. You are my deliverer and I thank you for the freedom I have in you. In Jesus' name I pray, amen."

Seek

Are you shackled?
Do you want to be free?
Identify what is holding you
back and cry out for God's
help.

Speak

In Jesus' name, I declare that every snare in my life has been broken. I am free to love God and live for him.

....

....

....

....

....

....

....

Go further

Psalm 107, Galatians 5:1, Luke 4:18-19

"Why am I discouraged? Why is my heart so sad? I will put my hope in God! I will praise him again — my savior and my God!"

PSALM 42:11 NLT

A VALLEY OF DRY BONES

*I*t's easy to fall into hopelessness and despair when it seems life has passed you by. A womb that remained barren, a relationship that never blossomed, a career that never took off the way you expected—your dreams shriveled and dry.

"Can these dry bones live?"

Ezekiel looked around him at the dry bones covering the valley floor. God had brought him to this place, but he was hesitant to answer God's question. "O Sovereign Lord," he replied. "You alone know the answer to that."

"Speak," God said in response to Ezekiel's noncommittal answer. "Speak to these bones and say, 'Dry bones, hear the word of the Lord!… Look! I am going to breathe into you and make you live again!'" (Ezekiel 37).

How impossible those words must have seemed to Ezekiel. And yet, he stirred his faith and obeyed. He spoke God's word, and suddenly, there was a rattling noise all across that valley as the bones came together, and then muscles and tendons and skin covered the bones.

Anticipation permeated the air—a trembling, an expectation, a hope. The miracle wasn't finished yet. God commanded Ezekiel to speak again. "Breath of God from the four winds, come and breathe life again into these dry bones!"

A mighty gasp echoed across the valley as the wind blew and LIFE came. The valley of death was now a valley of life. What was once seemingly beyond hope was alive! Living and breathing and strong.

What have you let dry up and die? God's promises are true and he is faithful. Listen for the word of the Lord and speak. Speak to your dreams, speak to your disappointments, speak to your soul. "Hope live! Faith arise! Breath of God, come breathe into the dry bones of my life!"

Pray

> *"God, help me believe again in all your goodness.
> I commit my dreams and hopes into your hand, and
> I speak life to them now. Come, O breath of God!"*

Seek

What dreams have you let die?
Are they within God's will?
Listen to the Lord and then
speak his words over your
dreams.

Speak

I speak the breath of God over every dream and situation in my life.
Live now!

Go further

Ezekiel 37:1-14, Isaiah 43:18-19,
Psalm 43:5, John 12:49-50

"...those who hope in the Lord will renew their strength. They will soar on wings like eagles; they will run and not grow weary, they will walk and not be faint."

ISAIAH 40:31 NIV

DAY 20

REST AND RECOVER

*A*re you feeling beat up? So often we think God is looking over our lives and saying, "buck up." Pull yourself up by your bootstraps and get moving.

There may be times in your life when that is precisely what you need to do. Stop the pity party, quit complaining and move on. You can feel a Holy Spirit "kick in the pants" and you realize you've got to pull yourself together and get back to living.

But sometimes we are called to come away, to rest and recover. To step away from the fray and be still before the Lord. Psalm 46 speaks to those moments in time when all you need to do is let God be God and receive his strength and rejuvenation for your soul.

"Come, behold the works of the Lord… He makes wars cease to the end of the earth; He breaks the bow and cuts the spear in two… Be still and know that I am God" (Psalm 46:8, 9, 10 NKJV).

You may feel like you've been in a war zone. The bruises and scrapes on your soul are real. You've been fighting the Lord's battles: standing up for righteousness, praying and interceding for God's will in your life or others', reaching out to the lonely and lost. Or, you've been merely working your crazy schedule to make ends meet or get your kids to soccer practice or take care of an aging parent.

You're tired and weary. You feel like you should be chiding yourself for not wanting to go on, but if you listen closely, you'll hear the Lord's voice saying, "Be still. Come away and rest for a while."

There will be other battles to fight, more victories to be won. But for now, in the greenness of this valley, in the richness of his presence, rest and recover.

Pray

"God, I confess that I am tired. I ask you to come and restore my soul, renew my strength. In Jesus' name, amen."

Seek

What is wearing you out?
Commit it to the Lord and listen for his voice. Perhaps there is a way to relieve this stress in your life.

Speak

When I am weary, God renews my strength. In him, I am strong.

Go further

Luke 9:10, 2 Corinthians 4:7-9, Galatians 6:9

"Do not despise these small beginnings, for the Lord rejoices to see the work begin..."

ZECHARIAH 4:10 NLT

A PLUMB LINE — JUDGMENT OR RESTORATION?

What is God doing in your life? Sometimes we lose forward movement in our lives because we misunderstand what the Lord is doing. Being passed over for a promotion may not be God's rejection but rather his intervention towards a new and better job. A relationship that hasn't worked out the way you hoped could be God's protection.

A plumb line is a tool used in construction to check the straightness of a wall. In Amos 7:7, God used a plumb line to check the righteousness of his people. He had endured enough of their sinful ways. Judgment was coming.

The second time a plumb line appears in the Bible is in Zechariah. The once-beautiful temple of Jerusalem was in ruins, demolished and destroyed by enemy forces. The people were rebuilding, led by Zerubbabel and guided by the prophets Haggai and Zechariah. It was a daunting task and the opposition was fierce.

God was pleased to see the reconstruction begin and encouraged Zechariah in a vision, "Do not despise these small beginnings, for the Lord rejoices to see the plumb line in Zerubbabel's hand" (Zechariah 4:10 NLT). The people had captured God's vision for their future. It was a momentous time in the nation's history.

Has God come to you with a plumb line? Before you assume that judgment is coming, consider the possibility that God may have a reconstruction project in mind. Perhaps he's come to rebuild where you've been torn down or restore areas in your life that have suffered demolition at the hands of an enemy. Or perhaps he's building something new, something extraordinary, something he's been dreaming about for a long time.

This is momentous! There may be hard work ahead, but I encourage you to rejoice in the revelation of what God is doing in your life. Rejoice with him, even as he rejoices to see the work begin. Something new is on the horizon.

Pray

> *"God, thank you for your work in my life! I believe that something new and good is on the horizon, and I commit to working with you on this reconstruction project. In Jesus' name!"*

Seek

What areas in your life need God's restoration?
Is it time for a reconstruction project? Rejoice in the process and encourage yourself that something new is coming.

I believe something new is on the horizon. God is at work in my life.

Go further

Isaiah 58:11-12, Luke 5:17, 1 Chronicles 12:32

"Blessed is the man who trusts in the Lord, whose confidence is in him."

JEREMIAH 17:7 BSB

DAY 22

WHO DO YOU BELONG TO?

*H*ave you ever seen two kids squabble on a playground, pushing each other around until one finally cries out, "My dad can beat your dad!"? It's a classic scene played out repeatedly in movies and TV.

Who do you belong to? When the enemy pushes you around, who do you align your life with? Where does your confidence lie?

God is compassionate to all. He shows his kindness to everyone, even those outside the faith, with the hope that it will lead them to repentance and faith in him. However, the Bible is filled with promises especially for God's people. Just like you take care of your family, as a good Father, God is watching over his kids. He is the Good Shepherd!

"I am the good shepherd; I know my sheep and my sheep know me, just as the Father knows me and I know the Father—and I lay down my life for the sheep" (John 10:14-15 NIV).

Unfortunately, this doesn't mean your life is "bully-proof." The Bible says the devil is always on the prowl, looking for someone to intimidate and devour. But if you grasp the concept of sonship, then when the enemy rushes at you like a bully, you're able to push back with a "my dad can beat your dad" kind of mentality.

Take a moment now and let this truth soak into your soul. It's critical to your well-being and your ability to overcome obstacles and persevere when your faith is challenged. Don't allow the enemy to stall you and hold you back from God's good purposes for your life. Remember whose you are.

You are the Lord's. You belong to him. And he takes care of his own. In that truth there is rest, comfort, and strength to persevere in life's journey. Don't let the enemy bully you around.

Pray

"God, I declare that I am yours! You are my heavenly Father and I trust you to protect me in every situation. I align my life with yours. In Jesus' name, amen."

Seek

Is there an area in your life where you have felt bullied?
Push back with the promises of God and ask the Lord to intervene for you today.

The enemy cannot bully me around. I belong to God.

2 Timothy 1:12, 2 Timothy 2:19,
Psalm 1:1, Jeremiah 17:7

"Intelligent people are always open to new ideas. In fact, they look for them."

PROVERBS 18:15 NLT

EVALUATE AND ADJUST

*W*hat do you do when things don't work out as planned? Are you open to new ideas? Determination and tenacity are virtues to cultivate, but there comes a point when determination turns into blind stubbornness and tenacity into hard-headedness.

The Bible says that in a multitude of counselors there is safety (Proverbs 11:14). If your well-thought-out plan is failing, are you open to allowing others to speak into your life? Are you open to adjusting your plan or taking a different route?

The exodus of the Israelites out of Egypt is a good example. When Pharoah finally let the people go, God did not lead them the shortest way to the promised land. The short route would have taken them right through the heart of enemy territory! Instead, he took them the longer route. "For God said, 'If they face war, they might change their minds and return to Egypt'" (Exodus 13:17 NIV).

Things change. People, culture, politics—disruptions happen that can shift a whole society. Often change is far beyond our control and, for better or worse, can affect the trajectory of our lives. Your plan may have been fail-safe, but then the unanticipated happens. Or it could simply be that you miscalculated in your planning.

Now what? It takes humility to take a step back and objectively evaluate what's working and what's not, but it's necessary if you're going to continue moving forward in God. It takes confidence in God's good plan for your life to seek counsel from others and ask for their input.

Remember the tenacity and determination we talked about earlier? You're going to need to draw on those strengths to accommodate the unexpected while maintaining your objective.

Be open to a new way. If your plans have gone awry, be willing to evaluate and adjust your path as necessary for a plan that ultimately will bring more glory to God.

Pray

> *"God, I commit my way to you. I know you have a good plan for my life and I seek out your help and counsel for my success. In Jesus' name, amen."*

Seek

Who are the people in your life that you can trust for godly counsel?
List them here, then reach out and ask them for input on your current situation or a future plan.

I am open to new ideas. In fact, I seek them out!

Go further

Proverbs 24:6, Proverbs 15:22, Proverbs 16:3

"*I am convinced that nothing can ever separate us from his love.*"

ROMANS 8:38 NLT

HAVE YOU DISQUALIFIED YOURSELF?

*H*ave you resigned yourself to a dark, never-ending valley? A valley can be many things, but perhaps for you, it's a prison you have willingly entered. You've pronounced judgment on your sins, pulled the bars closed on your life, and tossed the key.

What have you done? What evil deed resigned you to this fate? What do you feel has disqualified you so entirely that you have entered this state of suspension—suspending life, suspending love?

There is nothing that can separate you from the love of God. There is no sin so dark that the blood of Jesus cannot cover.

Consider Paul. As a young man, he watched over the clothes of Stephen's accusers as they stoned him to death. He then became a deadly persecutor of the early church (Acts 7:58). It mirrored the horrific tales you hear in today's news when a church is attacked, its pastor and members beaten or killed or imprisoned.

Or consider Peter, an apostle, one of the 12 who was side by side with Jesus for three and a half years. Yet when Peter was confronted concerning his alliance with the Lord, he denied it. With Jesus but a few yards away and Peter in his line of sight, three times Peter denied even knowing the man (Luke 23:60–62).

Both of these men could easily be disqualified. Sinners beyond saving. And yet...

God apprehended Paul and gave him a mission to preach salvation to the Gentiles. And Peter quickly found his way to repentance and forgiveness, becoming a bold leader of the early church. He was eventually martyred for his faith.

There is no sin that Jesus' blood cannot cover. A call and a purpose is waiting out there for you, beyond the walls of your self-constructed prison. Receive your forgiveness and pick up the mantle of God's plan for your life. Walk out of your valley and live.

Pray

*"God, I confess my sin and I seek your forgiveness.
I believe you have a plan for my life and I embrace it now,
through the blood and the name of Jesus Christ, amen."*

Seek

Are you prolonging your valley?
What do you feel has disqualified
you from serving the Lord? Today,
seek God's forgiveness and mercy.
Walk in the plan he has for your life.

The blood of Jesus covers my sin.
Nothing can separate me from God's love.

Go further

Psalm 139:7-12, Romans 8:31-38, Acts 2:37-39

"Come to me, all
you who are weary and
burdened, and I will
give you rest."

MATTHEW 11:28 NIV

P L A N T   A   G A R D E N
I N   T H I S   V A L L E Y

*I*t was contrary to everything the Israelites believed. They had been overpowered and carried away to Babylon. Now they were captives in a foreign land—unsettled, uneasy, and looking for a way to escape. This was not their home; it was not where they belonged.

And then the word of the Lord came to them through the prophet Jeremiah. "Build homes, and plan to stay. Plant gardens, and eat the fruit you produce... Multiply! Do not dwindle away!'" (Jeremiah 19:5-6 NLT).

In other words, make the most of this time in Babylon. Don't be in too big of a hurry to leave.

Sometimes, God may call you to dwell in your valley. To settle in a bit and plant some roots. To enjoy rest and reprieve from your travels. To embrace the moment as a God-ordained time to heal and get stronger, a time to regain vision for the future.

If God is speaking that message to your soul, then relax. Breathe. Look around and explore ways to be fruitful even while you recover from a loss or a stressful season of life. Build something of value, plant seeds of goodness, and taste the sweetness of the harvest.

As you rest in the safety of this valley, remember that you have a future. Don't allow yourself or your vision to dwindle away... but instead, use this time to multiply, to dream, to look ahead to what's next.

It's within the same passage of scripture in Jeremiah that God offered reassurance and encouragement to his people: "'For I know the thoughts that I think toward you,' says the Lord, 'thoughts of peace and not of evil, to give you a future and a hope'" (Jeremiah 29:11 NKJV).

The time will come when you'll pick up your walking stick and continue your journey. You'll be stronger and wiser and ready for the future God has in mind for your life. For now, look for ways to make this valley and this moment fruitful.

Pray

"God, I receive your rest. Please heal me and strengthen me. Show me how to be fruitful in this season. In Jesus' name, amen."

Seek

In what areas of your life do you need rest and healing?
Receive the strengthening of the Lord now.

Speak

God is thinking of me. In him, I have a future and a hope.

Go further

Psalm 127:2, Ecclesiastes 3:1-8, Jeremiah 29:1-14

"'For nothing is impossible with God.'"

LUKE 1:37 NLT

WHAT DO YOU HAVE
IN YOUR HOUSE?

Ever feel like the walls are closing in and there's no way out? You're desperate for a path through the dire situation, but you are stuck. Whatever you're facing, if you stir your faith to see with spiritual eyes, there is one simple question that can carve the way out of your seemingly unsolvable problem.

What do you have in your house?

In the days of the prophet Elisha, there was a widow whose husband had passed, leaving her and her two sons destitute and in debt. The creditors were at her door, threatening to take the sons as slaves. She cried out to Elisha for help, and he responded with a question. "'What do you have in the house?'

"Nothing at all, except a flask of olive oil,' she replied. And Elisha said, 'Borrow as many empty jars as you can from your friends and neighbors. Then go into your house with your sons and shut the door behind you. Pour olive oil from your flask into the jars, setting each one aside when it is filled'" (2 Kings 4:2-4 NLT).

In faith, she gathered the jars. And then she poured... She poured from that flask of oil, miraculously filling jar after jar until there were no more jars to fill. Then she sold the oil, paid off her debts, and had enough money left over to support her family.

God can use anything to work a miracle. Take a look around. Spiritually and physically, take an inventory. Is there something you consider ordinary or inconsequential that, when placed in the Lord's hands, could become your provision, your way forward?

- A talent you haven't tapped into
- An opportunity you've pushed aside
- An item on your shelves
- A spiritual weapon of prayer that you've not taken out of its sheath?

Whatever your dilemma, big or small, prayerfully consider and take inventory. Listen for God's wisdom and insight. What do you have in your house?

Pray

> "God, I bring my situation before you.
> I ask for your intervention and I look to you
> for divine provision. Help me see my way through,
> in Jesus' name, amen."

Seek

What situation seems impossible to you right now?
What do you have in your house? Take an inventory and listen for the Lord's voice. Your answer may be in your hand already.

Nothing is impossible with God!
He is my way through this situation.

Go further

2 Kings 4:1-7, Matthew 15:29-39, Philippians 4:19

"With God's help we will do mighty things..."

PSALM 108:13 NLT

DREAM

*M*oving forward in God means one step in front of another. Always forward, always focused. But in today's culture it's easy to get distracted and lose that focus and forward movement. We slosh around in the barrage of social media, news streams and Netflix, compounded by the battle of keeping the house clean or commuting to work or prepping for a Zoom meeting.

Remember when you used to dream? To imagine what could be? Thoughts sketched out on a napkin or brainstormed with a friend… But if you're honest with yourself, you'd have to admit that if you're even moving towards that dream, it's a slow crawl at best.

You've lost your focus, lost your purpose, maybe even lost your hope for the dream.

Perhaps it's weariness. You grew tired, stopped to rest, and just never got moving again. Perhaps you lost your support—your friend or cheerleader—and you haven't had the heart to rally yourself. Maybe you're just plain old surrounded by too many naysayers. And now you've lost your zeal for the vision of greatness you once held close to your soul.

Whatever the reason, life without a dream is not the way God has called you to live. God has called you to live a big life. A life of anticipation and expectation. A life of undertaking something beyond yourself while trusting God and his power within you to bring your impossible dream into reality.

I've heard it said that if your dream is something you can accomplish on your own, then it's not God. He is the God who can do more than you can ask or imagine, beyond the wildest thing you might even dare to hope for.

If you've lost your forward momentum, check your dream gauge. Clear the distractions, pick up your hope, and imagine what could be. Attach your faith to the vision and start dreaming again. With God's help, you can do mighty things.

Pray

"God, help me to keep moving forward.
Help me to dream again! I commit my dream into your hands,
and I believe that with your help all things are possible.
In Jesus' name, amen."

Seek

What has gotten in the
way of your dream?
How can you rekindle your
zeal to keep your forward
movement? Write down a
next step here.

_____

_____

_____

_____

_____

_____

_____

Speak

With God's help, I will do mighty things!

_____

_____

_____

_____

_____

_____

_____

_____

Go further

Hebrews 11:1, Ephesians 3:20, Mark 9:23

"If you wait for perfect conditions, you will never get anything done."

ECCLESIASTES 11:4 NLT

WHAT ARE YOU WAITING FOR?

*Y*our vision is renewed. You're beginning to dream again—and yet, if someone were to chart your progress, you've hardly moved an inch. Why?

What's holding you back? Doubt? Laziness? Fear? It may be a mixture of all three. You've got a plan, mapped out your goals, maybe even thought through the steps it will take to get there. And yet… you haven't moved. Haven't even started.

You may be able to justify your holding pattern by recounting your busy schedule or the lousy cold that set you back. Or perhaps doubt has crept in. If you wait until conditions are perfect, you will never move forward. Or as another version of scripture reads, "He who observes the wind will not sow, and he who regards the clouds will not reap" (Ecclesiastes 11:4 NKJV).

It's like a farmer standing at the edge of his field with good seed in his hand, but the wind is blowing in and it may storm… so he doesn't sow. Doesn't take the action to plant the seeds that will guarantee his future.

Or, maybe he does get the seed in the ground and now it's harvest time, but he's concerned about the clouds overhead. He misses his opportunity to reap because he was waiting for the perfect sunshiny day. And the crops sit in the field unharvested, the proverbial fruit rotting on the vine through the rain and snow of winter.

He wonders why life always seems so hard, why he lives on the edge of poverty, why his neighbor can afford a shiny new tractor while he limps along with the rusty one that's always in need of repair. He kicks the dog, yells at his wife or kids, maybe even shakes his fist at God for his lot in life.

If you wait for perfect conditions, you will never get anything done.

If you're held back by fear or overwhelmed by the task ahead, take one step at a time. Consider doable, actionable steps and then start walking. Don't wait. Start now. Do something that counts toward the dream today.

Pray

"God, forgive me for letting circumstances
become an excuse for inactivity. Help me trust you
and take action towards the good things you have for me.
In Jesus' name, amen."

Seek

**What dream has God put in
your heart?**
If you've let excuses or fear
hold you back, determine
one thing you can do today
to move towards that dream.

Speak

I am not swayed by circumstances. I trust God
and his timing for what he has called me to do.

Go further

Proverbs 22:13, John 4:35, Philippians 4:13

"The steps of the godly are directed by the Lord. He delights in every detail of their lives. Though they stumble, they will not fall, for the Lord holds them by the hand."

PSALM 37:23-24 NLT

NEXT STEPS

*H*ow are you doing? You may have started this journey with a bit of uncertainty, but hopefully you're beginning to understand the importance of living a life of purpose and vision. Although you may encounter opposition along the way, the Christian life can be a fulfilling walk of faith. But what if you don't know the next step to take? Where do you go from there?

Abraham was well settled in his hometown of Haran when God called him and set him on a journey beyond the imagination. He had the promise of God's blessing if he would go, but he didn't know where he was going. The only directive he had was to pack up and move out.

Then the Lord told Abram, 'Leave your country, your relatives, and your father's house, and go to the land that I will show you'" (Genesis 12:1 NLT).

When you don't have a clear picture of the path ahead, it's easy to default to inactivity, hesitating to take the steps that can move you out of your current situation and into a better one. Your life may not be perfect, but it's what you know and the thought of change is intimidating.

Abraham is known as the father of faith because he believed God and took those steps into his future, despite the uncertainties. He didn't quite know what lay ahead, but he had the promise of God that it would be good.

Can you hear God calling? Can you hear his voice coaxing you out of your valley and into a land of blessing? Your path may not be clear-cut, but if you desire to live for God, then forward is the only direction for you to choose.

Put your uncertainties into his hand and trust his guidance. There is blessing ahead for you!

Pray

> *"God, help me to believe in your good plan for my life. I trust you to lead and guide me as I move out of my valley and into your blessings. In Jesus' name, amen."*

Seek

As you look to your future, what are you uncertain about? What are you sure about relating to that same situation? Bring them both before the Lord and listen for his next steps.

Speak

My steps are directed by the Lord.
I can move forward because he holds my hand.

Go further

Psalm 31:24, Psalm 73:23-24,
James 1:5-8, Matthew 4:19-20

"I pray that your hearts will be flooded with light so that you can understand the wonderful future he has promised to those he called."

EPHESIANS 1:18 NLT

LOOK AHEAD

*H*ave you ever been in a situation where you see God's abundant blessing on your home, your work, and your life, and yet you feel there's something more? It's a sense of longing, and sometimes you don't even know what you're longing for, but you're not content to settle.

call it a divine discontent, a sense in your spirit that God is calling you higher and further. There is an inner feeling that a better future awaits just on the other side of this valley, something wonderful beyond your current here and now. If you squint, you can imagine the breathtaking mountains ahead.

The apostle Paul prayed for the believers in Ephesus that the eyes of their hearts would be opened; that they would be enlightened to the hope and future they have in God—the "riches of his glorious inheritance" (Ephesians 1:18 NIV).

When I feel unsettled, I first conduct a heart-check to ensure my restlessness isn't a product of an ungrateful heart. I thank God for his goodness and all the many ways he loves and cares for me.

Then I ask him to open my eyes and show me what lies beyond my current sphere, what I can't see with my natural eyes. What am I missing? What is he calling me to? How can I step towards it?

If you're feeling unsettled, go to God with a thankful heart and ask him for eyes to see what's ahead. Ask for his light to shine into your heart and reveal what it will take to enter that promising future. Maybe now is simply the time to pray and believe what he is showing you. Or, perhaps it's time to prepare with additional schooling or a maneuvering of your finances or other details in your life to accommodate what's ahead.

Be thankful for the here and now but press into what lies ahead. The timing may not be quite yet, but your future is bright when you are on his path.

Pray

"God, flood my heart with your light!
Thank you for your goodness. Help me
see into the good future you have for me.
In Jesus' name, amen."

Seek

What does your heart sense for your future?

Is there preparation involved? Pray and seek God for what you should do now to be prepared for what's to come.

I open my heart to receive God's light.
I have a wonderful future in God.

Go further

"Enter his gates with thanksgiving; go into his courts with praise."

PSALM 100:4 NLT

FUEL FOR THE JOURNEY

Thankfulness. It's like a spiritual boost for your life, an energy drink for the journey. Thankfulness can supercharge you when you feel drained. It can be the wind in your sails moving you onward, the lift in your spirit carrying you upward.

A thankful heart can sweep you up out of the mundane and into the marvelous life-giving presence of God. And in his presence, there is everything you need.

If you're hopeless, he is hope.
If you're weary, he is strength.
If you're lost, he is the way.

Even on the bleakest days, there is always something to praise God for, but it takes discipline to incorporate gratitude into your life. It may be as basic as saying thanks over a meal or beginning each morning with a prayer of gratitude for the mercy of a new day.

You might even list out things from yesterday that you are thankful for today. Did you have a good workday? Did you sleep well? Did you and a friend or spouse have a good conversation about a topic you've been putting off for way too long?

If you're in a difficult time, then yes, pour out your heart before God, but begin by thanking him for who he is and what he has brought you through. Psalm 150 is an amazing display of boisterous, unhindered praise and thanksgiving, with the final admonishment, "Let everything that has breath praise the Lord."

Thankfulness will carry you a long way through this journey of life.

"Give thanks to the Lord, for he is good! His faithful love endures forever. Who can list the glorious miracles of the Lord? Who can ever praise him half enough?" (Psalm 106:1–2 NLT).

Pray

"God, I thank you for all you have done for me. Help me cultivate a heart of gratitude that will fuel me for life's journey. In Jesus' name, amen."

Seek

What are you thankful for?
What can you praise God for? List ways that you can cultivate a heart of gratitude in your life.

Speak

Thank you, God, for your goodness!
I thank you for another day to live.

Go further

Philippians 4:6-7, Psalm 62:8, Luke 17:11-19

"Don't be impatient
for the Lord to act!
Travel steadily along
his path."

PSALM 37:34 NLT

S L O W   B U T   S T E A D Y

*G*od has birthed an idea in you. Whether it was a word, a dream, or an idea that came to you as you were driving down the highway or watching your kids play soccer, you finally have a vision for your future. You're high on the epiphany and super excited.

Now what? You're ready to get moving out of the *now* and into the *new* and you're wondering—*how can we speed this thing along*?

Abraham had a promise from God. A promised son—a child from his loins who would carry on the family name. The Bible says Abraham believed God and the Lord declared him righteous because of his faith. Can you imagine him sharing the news with Sarah? Filled with adrenaline, he was already planning this child's future.

Abraham was 75 years old when he received his promise from God. Nine years later, impatience got the better of them. Looking at the facts of the situation, Sarah suggested her servant Hagar to him and Abraham quickly agreed.

Hagar gave birth and Abraham became the father of Ishmael. Although God blessed him, Ishmael was not Abraham's promised future. It wasn't until Abraham was 100 years old that Sarah gave birth to Isaac. That's 25 years from the spoken promise to the actual fulfillment.

I love the simplicity of the Bible when it records in Genesis 21:1, "Then the Lord did exactly what he had promised. Sarah became pregnant, and she gave a son to Abraham in his old age."

The Bible says God's promises are "yes and amen." What God says, he will fulfill. Your part is to trust and believe. Unfortunately, it's easy to fall prey to doubt or impatience when things move more slowly than you hoped.

When you're tempted to "push things along," stop and consider the faithfulness of God. Slow but steady, keep trusting and stay the course of the good things God has for you.

"Dear God, help me trust your promises to me. I believe that you are faithful. Help me stay the course and not push your timeline. In Jesus' name, amen."

Seek

What do you believe is in your future?
Are you walking in faith towards it, or have you grown impatient? Commit your dream anew to God today.

My future is secure in God.
My faith is grounded in his faithfulness to me.

Go further

2 Corinthians 1:20, Genesis 15-21,
Hebrews 11:1, Romans 4:16-22

"See, I am doing a new thing! Now it springs up; do you not perceive it? I am making a way in the wilderness and streams in the wasteland..."

ISAIAH 43:19 NIV

ARE YOU TRYING TO RECREATE THE PAST?

*W*e all have favorite memories, moments in time we'd love to relive. But if you dwell in the past too much you can miss the new that God wants to do in your life.

f you're ever tried to recreate that first date with your spouse, recapture the wonder of a family vacation when the kids were little, or relive a childhood memory of an ice cream cone at a favorite place, then you've probably felt the frustration of a date or trip or moment gone wrong. Life and people have moved on.

Your spouse is preoccupied with a problem at work. The kids want to go off and do their own thing now instead of hanging with the parents, and let's face it, that ice cream cone just doesn't taste the way it did when you were eight.

I've been there. I've imagined recreating a date night with my husband like we enjoyed a few years ago. But reality hit me as I was dreaming/scheming to recreate the moment. Time has taken over. The restaurant has changed hands. My husband's concept of a relaxing evening has changed. I've changed.

I realized I needed to let go of trying to recreate something from the past and find ways to create new memories. Find a new favorite restaurant, a fresh way to spend time together. Forge a new path and fill my memory bank with something new. Quit living in the past and start looking towards the future.

Sometimes beautiful moments will surprise you. Often they come through letting go of the past so you can anticipate and look forward to what's ahead.

God has a future and a hope for you. He's all about new! New covenant, new mercies, new hearts, new creations. Be thankful for the memories. Hold those special moments in your heart, but reach into your future and build something new.

Pray

> *"God, I thank you for the good memories I have,*
> *but I don't want to live in the past. Help me move*
> *towards the new and good future you have for me.*
> *In Jesus' name, amen!"*

Seek

What special new thing would you like to do?

Make plans now to create a new memory for yourself, your family or a friend.

Speak

I embrace the new thing God is doing in my life!

Go further

Luke 5:36-38, 2 Corinthians 5:17,
Ephesians 4:22-24, Revelation 21:1

"If you need wisdom—if you want to know what God wants you to do—ask him, and he will gladly tell you..."

JAMES 1:5 NLT

DAY 34

THE VALLEY OF DECISION

Sometimes life is black and white. In those cases, decisions are easy to make. It's the gray areas that are tough and can leave you wavering in a "valley of decision." Do you take a promotion that means a bigger salary but less time with family, or do you wait for a better opportunity? Do you opt for adoption or continue to wait and see? Do you send your kids to public school or homeschool them this year?

"Thousands upon thousands are waiting in the valley of decision. It is there that the day of the Lord will soon arrive" (Joel 3:14 NLT).

This scripture references a future showdown of sorts when all the armies of the world will gather in the valley of Jehoshaphat. On one side, those who oppose the Lord will face a terrifying moment of judgment. But for those on the Lord's side, the prophet Joel describes God as a "refuge for his people" (Joel 3:16).

It's a powerful visual of a clear delineation between God's people and the world. For us, it's an opportunity to determine how we will approach life. What side of the valley will you stand on?

Will you look to the Lord in your decision-making or will you rely on the world's ways—the mentality of people in the breakroom or in line at the coffee shop? Joel describes God as a welcoming refuge. In the New Testament, James also describes God as approachable. He even says that God invites you to ask him for wisdom, with one word of caution:

"But when you ask him, be sure that you really expect him to tell you, for a doubtful mind will be as unsettled as a wave of the sea that is driven and tossed by the wind" (James 1:6 NLT). If you ask God for wisdom, expect him to answer. Receive the wisdom he gives without doubt and without wavering in the "valley of decision."

If your life has stalled because of indecision, check your faith and check your sources. You don't have to rely on the world's "wisdom." You can ask God and he will gladly direct your path!

Pray

"God, I ask for your wisdom concerning _____.
Lead me and guide me. I declare that I fully expect you
to answer and I trust your response. In Jesus' name, amen.

Seek

**What area do you need
wisdom in today?**
Ask, and believe God
for the answer.

I will not waver in unbelief.
I receive and believe God's wisdom for my life.

John 16:23-24, James 3:17, Psalm 25:1-2

"O Lord... You have hedged me behind and before and laid your hand upon me."

PSALM 139:1,5 NKJV

HEDGED IN

*I*t's easy to settle in your valley when you're afraid of moving forward. Maybe you tried to step out before and failed, or you are hesitant to leave the security of what you know. Why rock the boat?

Although it's important to be present in life, it's also important to practice forward-thinking. God has so much more in mind for you! You've got to find the courage to try something new, to step out of your comfort zone, to risk something to gain more. More love, more life, more joy.

If you never step beyond your status quo, you'll be the one at your high school reunion whose life stalled at graduation. You'll be the one carrying regrets or watching in envy as others pass you by with a better job, a closer family, a life well-lived and enjoyed.

But fear is real. I get it. The "what ifs" can drive you further and further back inside your hole, like the groundhog on Groundhog Day who hesitates to come out and live. Really live.

So how do we beat the fear? It boils down to trust and an understanding of who you are and what you mean to God.

"O Lord, You have searched me and known me. You have hedged me behind and before, and laid your hand upon me" (Psalm 139:1, 5 NKJV).

Hedged in. Imagine it. No matter how deep or dark your valley or circumstance, God before you, God behind you–hedging you in. Protecting, guarding, keeping. The thought of it awed the psalmist as he declared, "Such knowledge is too wonderful for me" (Psalm 139:6 NKJV).

You are secure in God. Life can be risky and yes, a little scary at times, but you are not alone. God will lead you. He will hold you. He has hedged you in, behind and before.

Pray

"God, I don't want life to pass me by!
Help me to push past my fears. I trust you
and thank you for hedging me in, behind and before.
In Jesus' name, amen."

Seek

What scares you?
Be honest with yourself and
with God, and grab hold of
new faith in his care for you.

Speak

I will not be afraid. God has hedged me in, behind and before!

_____

_____

_____

_____

_____

_____

_____

_____

_____

_____

Go further

Psalm 139, Matthew 8:23-27,
Psalm 56:3, Psalm 115:11

"Fan into flame the gift of God..."

2 TIMOTHY 1:6 NIV

FAN THE FLAME

*A*re you reconsidering this journey? Are you second-guessing yourself and your quest to move forward in God? Sometimes we need a little push, a little stirring up of our spirits to keep advancing.

Even Timothy, the apostle Paul's "son in the faith," needed fatherly encouragement to continue in the ministry God had given him. Maybe he had shrunk back after a bad experience or gotten weary or just lost his way. But Paul noticed something had changed in him and he wasn't about to see his son falter in the way.

"I remember your genuine faith, for you share the faith that first filled your grandmother Lois and your mother, Eunice. And I know that same faith continues strong in you. This is why I remind you to fan into flames the spiritual gift God gave you when I laid my hands on you" (2 Timothy 1:5-6 NLT).

He didn't leave it at that—a simple admonishment to keep the faith. Paul looked deeply into Timothy's heart. Timothy wasn't being lazy or non-committal. He was fearful and unsure. Like a wise father, Paul added, "For God has not given us a spirit of fear, but of power and of love and of a sound mind" (2 Timothy 1:7 NKJV).

Even the best of us can lose our zeal to serve the Lord. It takes sacrifice and commitment to walk through this earth as a disciple of Christ, shining your light and bringing real change to the world. You may have started strong, but now the fire is waning and you're ready to go back to a more comfortable life, an easier way.

This is your reminder that the world needs what you can offer as a disciple of Christ, someone who believes in the living God. Your co-worker with breast cancer needs to know that God still heals today. Your neighbor whose teenage son suffers from addiction needs a faith-filled person who will believe with them for deliverance. Your kids need an example, a plumb line life to follow when the world pushes and pulls at their Christian convictions.

Fan the flame, silence the fear, lay hold of God's power and love. Start believing again. Keep moving forward.

Pray

> "God, help me fan the flame of your spirit in my life!
> Give me strength and courage to move forward
> in your power and love. In Jesus' name, amen."

Seek

What has slowed you down?
Identify the source of fear or
intimidation. Then, find a way
to fan God's spirit within you to
conquer this with his power and
love and soundness of mind.

God has not given me a spirit of fear,
but one of power, love and self-discipline!

Go further

Luke 4:18-19, Matthew 5:14-16, Philippians 2:14-16

"How can you show me your faith if you don't have good deeds? I will show you my faith by my good deeds."

JAMES 2:18 NLT

NOT ALL ACTIVITY IS ACTION

Ever feel like you're spinning your wheels? Your schedule is packed but at the end of the day, it's hard to put your finger on what you accomplished. Nothing gained, no markers passed. Yet you're tired and ready to close your computer or flip on the TV and call it a day.

There's an old saying that not all activity is action. You may be crossing things off your list of to-do's but how much of that moves you towards your end goal? You can be deceived by busyness when what you're really doing is avoiding the down-and-dirty work it's going to take to advance your career, your relationships, your life through this valley.

It's like you're embodying the scripture in Ecclesiastes 1:2, "Vanity of vanities, all is vanity."

Moving forward in faith means setting measurable goals and then creating a plan to meet those goals. Advancement in a career is not easy. Greater fulfillment in a marriage or friendship takes commitment and vulnerability. Taking ground spiritually to advance God's kingdom in your life or another's requires tenacity, perseverance and often, serious spiritual warfare.

The Bible refers to the advancement of the Kingdom of Heaven as forceful. It doesn't come easy and it may not come quick. It takes deliberate action and it's something that "violent" people lay hold of (Matthew 11:12).

In other words, your little to-do list will probably not get the job done.

If you're tired of walking in circles, tired of going around that same bush–a career stall, relational conflict, or overwhelming debt–consider a new approach. Consider the action that will move you forward in life and into the fullness of all God has promised for those that believe. Let your faith shine with each step you take.

Pray

"God, help me walk in faith and prioritize my life
so that I am truly accomplishing good things.
I look to you for wisdom and grace, in Jesus' name, amen."

Seek

**What action will move you
toward your goals?**
Write down at least one thing
you can do today that is real
action and not just busy activity.

I am walking my faith out with action.

Go further

James 2:17-18, Hebrews 11:32-33, John 15:1-5

"Has the Lord redeemed you? Then speak out! Tell others he has redeemed you from your enemies."

PSALM 107:2 NLT

IS YOUR MUTE BUTTON ON?

*I*t's comforting to know that the Lord is "a mighty rock where I can hide" (Psalm 94:22). A shelter from the storms, a refuge from the enemy, a hiding place. There are moments in life when we need to escape from the stress and struggle of this world.

However, you can get yourself in trouble if you never come out of hiding. Like a child playing hide and seek, if you stay hidden away too long, your life becomes stuck on "mute." You're content to remain silent, to stay hidden—in fact, to never come out.

You can hear a friend or even the voice of the Lord urging you to "come out, come out, wherever you are" but there's something enamoring about staying hidden. It's like a gentle hush has come over your life and you kind of like it that way—no one's drama to deal with, no one to answer to. It's so serene here, you're becoming drowsy and drifting off to sleep...

Don't get me wrong; there are times to regroup and fall back into the refuge of God's rock, to linger in the quiet place. But stay there too long and you'll lose your purpose and your way forward. What began as a hiding place has turned into a trap of the enemy.

There is a time to come out of hiding and give the Lord the glory he deserves. A time to unmute yourself and tell the world all that the Lord has done. There is a time to shout his praise!

And if you're wondering just what to shout, shout if the Lord has saved you! Shout if he's protected you. Come out of your hiding place and tell the world about the goodness of the Lord. Don't allow your life to be muted.

Pray

> "God, I may have stayed too long under wraps.
> I acknowledge that you are God. Help me to
> speak forth your praise, in Jesus' name, amen!"

Seek

Has the enemy tried to mute your life?
In what areas do you feel like you've been silenced? Write out specific ways you can switch your voice back on.

I will not allow the enemy to mute my life.
I declare that the Lord is good! I shout his praise!

Go further

Psalm 100:1-3, Psalm 98:4-6, Matthew 5:13-15

"Jesus responded, 'Didn't I tell you that you would see God's glory if you believe?'"

JOHN 11:40 NLT

DAY 39

ANOTHER OPPORTUNITY TO BELIEVE

*H*ave you ever come to a bend in the road and hesitated? Unsure of the future, you stall in your tracks. There may be fear involved or a risk you're not prepared to take. Moving forward into the unknown can be intimidating if you're wary of what lies ahead.

The disciples hesitated and almost missed a miracle. They were with Jesus beyond the Jordan, safely out of reach from the Jewish authorities in Judea who were intent on killing Jesus. And then the news came from Judea that Lazarus was sick. His two sisters begged Jesus to come. They knew his healing touch could save their brother.

Although Jesus loved Martha, Mary, and Lazarus, he stayed where he was for two more days. The disciples didn't prod Jesus. They didn't urge him to go heal his friend. There was a price on Jesus' head in Judea and who knows what would happen to them if they went there!

Have you ever wondered what Jesus was thinking in those two days, knowing that Lazarus was dying? Was he hoping the disciples would rise out of their fear? Was he waiting for them to take the step of faith to go where they were needed? The life and death danger was very real, and when Jesus finally said, "Let's go," they still objected strongly.

Jesus replied, "'Lazarus is dead. And for your sake, I am glad I wasn't there, because this will give you another opportunity to believe in me...'" (John 11:14-15 NLT).

Another opportunity to believe. An occasion for the disciples to push past their fear and see the glory of God. A chance to see the dead raised to life!

What about you? Have you hesitated in your walk with God because of fear? Has doubt crept in? Is Jesus waiting on you?

The Christian walk is not always easy or comfortable. Sometimes Jesus calls us out of our fear to experience the miraculous. If fear is holding you back, let faith arise. Grab hold of "another opportunity to believe." There may be an incredible miracle just around the bend.

Pray

"God, help me to believe in you! Help me to trust you as I push all fear and doubt aside and take this next step forward in my life. In Jesus' name, amen."

Seek

Do you ever hesitate because of fear or doubt?
What area of life is most difficult to trust God with? Commit that to the Lord now and ask for renewed faith.

I will not shrink back because of fear.
I believe in God and I will walk forward in faith.

Go further

2 Corinthians 5:7, Hebrews 11:1, John 20:30-31

"Every valley shall be lifted up, and every mountain and hill made low... the glory of the Lord will be revealed, and all humanity together will see it."

ISAIAH 40:4-5 BSB

EVERY VALLEY PULLED UP

*W*hat's your valley? That's where we began this journey so many days ago, and now it's time to consider God's intention for the valleys of life. According to Isaiah 40, God's plan is to raise the valley and level it off so that all humanity will see his glory and encounter his goodness.

The verse before this refers to John the Baptist and his ministry, pointing the people of his day to Jesus. When asked by the Pharisees who he was, John the Baptist replied: "A voice of one calling, 'Prepare the way for the Lord in the wilderness; make a straight highway for our God in the desert'" (Isaiah 40:3 BSB).

God has decreed it: this valley shall be made a highway. Every area of oppression or depression will be lifted up. Your valley—your life—is meant to be a pathway for others to encounter the living God.

This is where prayer comes in. This is where spiritual warfare must be waged and won.

This is where you take God's word concerning this valley and declare to every force of darkness—every downward pull of oppression or depression that presses on your life—the spirit-inspired words that will bring your valley experience into line with God's plan to draw all men to himself.

Lives are at stake. Futures hang in the balance. Your valley must be conquered for others to have a level pathway, an easy entrance into God's presence.

Wage the spiritual battle. Speak to the valleys in your life. "Be lifted up! Depression, go! Every oppressive thing, get off me! I command a raising up of the ground of my life to become what God has ordained. I declare God's enabling power for me to become all that he has called me to."

May every valley in your life be pulled up because ultimately, your life is to be a highway for the Lord.

Pray

> *"God, help me fight through so that my life
> becomes a highway for others to encounter you!
> I command every valley in my life to be lifted up now,
> in the name of Jesus."*

Seek

**What is pressing down
on your life?**
Determine now to wage
spiritual warfare through prayer,
declaration, and praise to push
it off so you can be a highway
for God.

Speak

In Jesus' name, I speak to every area of oppression
or depression in my life to be lifted off.
I declare my life will be a highway for the Lord.

Go further

John 1:22-23, 1 Timothy 2:1-4, Hebrews 12:1-2

ACKNOWLEDGEMENTS

Special thanks to the team at The Giving Company and Family Christian. David Henriksen, John Crowe, Kobus Johnsen and others - you make it a joy to write for the Lord.

Thank you to my beautiful focus group friends, Linda Forbush, D'Lynn Watts, Lisa Millikin, Nathan and Jennifer Stuchenko, and also Sarah Schultz. Your insight was invaluable and so very appreciated.

And last but certainly not least, thank you to my husband Sam Woodworth and my wonderful kids, David, Sarah, Esther and Febe, and your families for your precious support of all my writing ventures.

May God be glorified in all our lives.

Laura Woodworth

ABOUT THE AUTHOR

_L_aura Woodworth is an award-winning writer-producer-director, script consultant, and development executive for Cooke Media Group in Los Angeles. She holds a B.A. in Ministerial Studies and completed UCLA's Professional Program in Producing. Her awards include the International Christian Film Festival's "Most Inspirational Short Film" and the Telly award-winning documentary, "Asia: The Great Wall and Beyond" of the TBN television series "Inexplicable." A contributor to FamilyChristian.com, iDisciple and Pure Flix Insider, she is also a YouVersion Partner with over 200,000 subscribers to her devotional plans.

Although Laura Woodworth grew up in church, it wasn't until she was 18 years old that she experienced the Living God in a real and tangible way. It changed her life forever and it's from that place of encounter and ongoing relationship with God that she writes.

For more inspirational resources visit LauraWoodworth.com.

IF YOU ENJOYED THIS BOOK, WILL YOU SHARE THE MESSAGE WITH OTHERS?

Leave a review online at Amazon or wherever you purchased this book. Every review matters and will help others experience God's power to move through their valley.

Mention the book on Facebook or Twitter or take a picture with it and post on Instagram. Tag me and I'll be sure to see it.

Recommend this book to friends or others in a small group or class.

Consider gifting a copy to someone you know who needs the transforming power of God to move forward on life's journey.

Thank you!

Laura Woodworth